TH POLE 80°

70°

IC

ARCTIC
CIRCLE

An International Wolf Center Book

WOLVES
OF THE HIGH ARCTIC

Photographs by L. David Mech

An International Wolf Center Book

WOLVES
OF THE HIGH ARCTIC

Photographs by L. David Mech

VOYAGEUR PRESS

All royalties from the sale of Wolves of the High Arctic *go to the International Wolf Center.*
For information about membership, contact
THE INTERNATIONAL WOLF CENTER
1396 Highway 169, Ely, Minnesota 55731
Phone 218-365-4695

Edited by Elizabeth Knight
Printed in Hong Kong
93 94 95 96 5 4 3 2

Library of Congress Cataloging-in-Publication Data
Wolves of the high Arctic / photography by L. David Mech.
p.   cm.

ISBN 0-89658-213-2
ISBN 0-89658-222-1 (pbk.)
1. Wolves—Arctic regions.   2. Wolves—Arctic regions—Pictorial
works.   3. International Wolf Center.   I. Mech, L. David.
II. International Wolf Center.
QL737.C22W649   1992
599.74'442—dc20   92-21714
CIP

Published by
VOYAGEUR PRESS, INC.
P.O. Box 338, 123 North Second Street
Stillwater, MN 55082 U.S.A.
From Minnesota and Canada 612-430-2210
Toll-free 800-888-9653

Voyageur Press books are also available at discounts for quantities for educational, fundraising, premium, or sales-promotion use. For details contact the marketing department. Please write or call for our free catalog of natural history publications.

The International Wolf Center dedicates *Wolves of the High Arctic* to

Tracy A. Weeks

"So that nothing is wasted in nature
or in love."

CONTENTS

THE INTERNATIONAL WOLF CENTER

Since humans first drew petroglyphs to record their observations, wolves have populated the art, the literature, and the culture of the planet. The howl of the wolf sends shivers of fascination and love or fear and distrust up the backs of people around the world. Hardly anyone treats the wolf with indifference.

In 1985, the wolf's relationships with other living creatures became the topic of a celebrated exhibit at the Science Museum of Minnesota. The six-thousand-square-foot, six-hundred-thousand-dollar display won awards, set attendance records, and eventually went on tour, to be viewed by millions around the United States and Canada.

The wolf enthusiasts who consulted in the creation of the exhibit began planning for its return to Minnesota. Dr. L. David Mech pulled together representatives from private, public, and professional groups to form the Committee for an International Wolf Center. The goal: a permanent home for the exhibit and an international center promoting public education about the endangered wolf. The site search for the nonprofit center ended in the geographical heart of the largest wolf population in the lower forty-eight states — in Ely, Minnesota. A temporary facility was established there, on the edge of the Boundary Waters Canoe Area Wilderness.

For five decades, gray wolf research conducted near Ely has informed the world about this dwindling species and has contributed to its repopulation in the north woods. Sigurd Olson, a world renowned naturalist, made the first noted studies in the 1930s. Milt Stenlund conducted a second wolf research project from 1948 to 1952. Dave Mech, of the U.S. Fish and Wildlife Service, and his colleagues have tracked and studied wolves in northern Minnesota since 1966. The foremost international expert in the field, Dr. Mech generously interprets his research for the International Wolf Center's educational programs and serves the board of directors as vice chair.

Visitors to the International Wolf Center see, touch, and hear the presence of the wolf. One can fly over a wolf pack or put on snow shoes and follow the predators' winter tracks. On warm Minnesota nights, children and adults join evening howling expeditions. Elderhostel groups learn how to track using the electronic technology of radio collars. Earthwatch volunteers assist in on-going wolf research. For those who cannot travel to Ely, nationally known speakers carry the story of the endangered wolf to schools and organizations around the country.

The new, million-dollar International Wolf Center in Ely will feature the "Wolves and Humans" exhibit and a live wolf pack. The facility, now under construction, will open in spring 1993.

Experts from around the world have contributed their knowledge to the museum and interpretive center. As the wolf center grows, it will expand with a zoological and research library. This clearing house of wolf-related information will draw from affiliated domestic and foreign colleges and universities, as well as from foundations and governments around the world.

Members of the International Wolf Center come from the fifty United States and twenty-two nations. All members receive a subscription to *International Wolf* magazine, an authoritative quarterly publication of lively features about wolves and wolf issues worldwide.

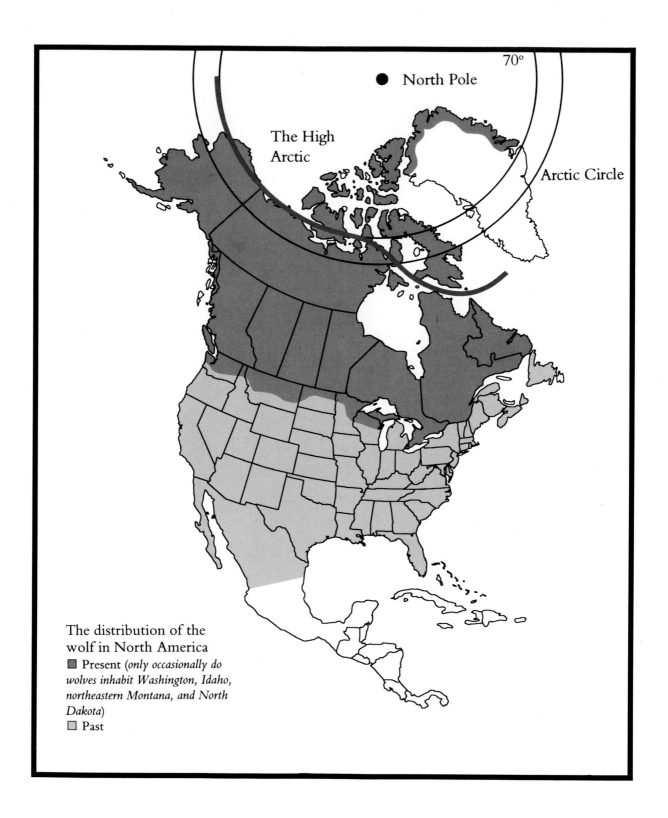

North Pole

70°

The High
Arctic

Arctic Circle

The distribution of the
wolf in North America

■ Present (*only occasionally do
wolves inhabit Washington, Idaho,
northeastern Montana, and North
Dakota*)
□ Past

AN INTERVIEW WITH L. DAVID MECH

Several large islands occupy the region between the north edge of continental North America and the North Pole. Although ice and snow permanently cover much of the area, parts of these islands become snowfree between mid-June and mid-August and support enough low-growing plants to feed musk-oxen, Peary caribou, and arctic hares. These creatures constitute the food supply for the white wolves who live in this place we call the High Arctic.

The High Arctic is mostly unsettled by people. The northernmost Inuit village nestles at about 75 degrees north latitude. This village of about one hundred people was built in the 1950s by the Canadian government, and Inuit from farther south were moved there. The only other year-round human outposts in the region include weather stations and a military base. All these settlements are relatively recent. And as a result, arctic wolves really have never been hunted or seriously pursued in most of the High Arctic, contrary to their counterparts throughout the rest of the northern hemisphere. This makes them relatively unafraid of any human beings they do run into. Rather than flee at the very scent of a human, they merely stand and gaze. In some areas, they can even be coaxed up close.

This lack of fear on the part of arctic wolves has allowed wolf biologist L. David Mech to befriend a pack of them and to learn many things he could not by working with wolves farther to the south for some thirty-three years. First with his article in *National Geographic* "At Home With the Arctic Wolf," and then with his *National Geographic* Explorer video "White Wolf" and the Voyageur Press book *The Arctic Wolf*, Mech has shared with the public his unique experience with these white wolves. Now, after having lived with this same pack for six summers, he shares more of his insight into this pack through this book of photographs.

Through donating the use of these photos to the International Wolf Center and agreeing to be interviewed, Dave Mech provides an update on this wolf pack and gives us some background on the wolves of the High Arctic.

International Wolf Center (IWC) Administrator Mary Ortiz discussed wolves of the High Arctic with L. David Mech. Ms. Ortiz has been a staff member of the wolf center since 1987, playing an integral role in such vital educational activities as its speakers bureau, membership program, and *International Wolf* magazine.

* * *

IWC: Dr. Mech, why should anyone be interested in wolves of the High Arctic?

LDM: Well, it certainly is true that very few people ever get a chance to visit the High Arctic, much less observe arctic wolves, but the life of the arctic wolf is basically the same as the lives of wolves everywhere. The arctic wolf (*Canis lupus arctos*), a specialized race or subspecies of the gray wolf (*Canis lupus*), lives in the area along the northern edge of the North American continent and northward to the North Pole, as well as along the eastern and northern shores of Greenland. White coats and slightly shorter noses and ears distinguish these wolves from other races of the gray wolf. Although early scientists recognized five races of white wolves in this region, and five or six just to the south, the findings of modern wolf biology tend to imply that technically it is probably more accurate to think of all of the white wolves in the region as belonging to one or two races.

Some white wolves can be found as far south as Wood Buffalo National Park in northern Alberta, Canada, at a latitude of 60 degrees. At least one white wolf has been seen as far south as northern Minnesota. Because wolves sometimes disperse straight-line distances of over 550 miles, conceivably genes of the arctic wolf have found their way to Minnesota. On the other hand, most wolves south of about 70 degrees north latitude, which more or less borders the northern edge of continental North America, are gray or black. North of about 70 degrees, most if not all wolves are white.

Coat color is actually a very superficial characteristic with which to evaluate any species. The arctic wolf is a wolf. It's shaped like any other wolf, acts like any other wolf, travels like any other kind of wolf, breeds with any other kind of wolf, and behaves like any other wolf.

The arctic wolf's nose and ears are slightly shorter, probably to minimize their exposure to the intense cold and wind.

IWC: Then why is the arctic wolf so special to you?

LDM: Because the arctic wolf is the only kind of wolf that I, or any other biologist, have ever been able to observe closely and intimately on a day-to-day basis with any degree of consistency.

IWC: How close to these wolves have you been?

LDM: What I mean is, I've been able to live right with a pack of arctic wolves around their den for six summers now.

IWC: Why couldn't you do that with any other kind of wolf?

LDM: Because everywhere else in the world, except for in the High Arctic, wolves have been so persecuted by human beings for so long that they are extremely shy and elusive. If a person comes near their den, the wolves may move right out. If a wolf smells or hears or otherwise detects a human, it immediately runs away, before the human ever gets a chance to see it. As you can imagine, such wolves are very difficult to study. Putting radio collars on them and studying their movements via radio signal was the only way I could observe wolves up close anywhere else in the world, except by raising them in captivity and studying them in enclosures.

IWC: What's wrong with that?

LDM: You certainly can learn some interesting information by studying captive wolves. However, the captive situation itself prevents studies of many kinds, for example, of their daily activity pattern, their movements, their hunting behavior, and all other aspects of their life that would be restricted or modified by a fence.

IWC: And the arctic wolves are so tolerant that you actually could live with them?

LDM: In most of the High Arctic, wolves live so far from human beings that they have not been hunted or persecuted — ever. They are basically unafraid of people. I know of one biologist who fed a wild arctic wolf a candy bar from his hand. In another instance, a wild arctic wolf licked the face of a photographer who was down on his knees to photograph the wolf. An ornithologist once grabbed a pup from a wild arctic wolf pack and carried it back to his tent; the pup's mother followed at the ornithologist's heels and slept outside the tent all night. One of the pups I lived with came up and untied my bootlace.

IWC: Was that pup a member of the pack you wrote about in *National Geographic* and in your book *The Arctic Wolf: Living with the Pack*?

LDM: Yes, and of the same pack we featured in our *National Geographic* Explorer video "White Wolf."

IWC: When did all this begin?

LDM: I first visited the High Arctic in April 1986 and met the pack then. There were seven adults. A companion and I had snowmobiles flown up for helping gather material for an article about the High Arctic for *National Geographic* magazine. When we saw that the wolves did not flee from us, even when we approached on snowmobiles, I realized what a wealth of information I could gather by befriending this pack.

I did that by trying to stay with the wolves most of the time so they got entirely used to us, by never scaring them, by tossing them little tidbits as we traveled with them, and by always backing off if they ever acted upset or disturbed with us. When I saw how well they responded, I vowed to return in summer and to try to locate their den.

IWC: And as we know from your earlier work, you did find the den and began living with the wolves.

LDM: Yes, with the adults and their pups.

IWC: How many pups were there?

LDM: Well, in 1986 there were six.

IWC: Thirteen wolves in the pack! How did you keep track of them all?

LDM: I really couldn't tell the pups apart, but I could the adults. There was Mom, the mother of the pups; Shaggy, a subordinate female probably two or three years old; Mid-Back, a young but very dominate female; Alpha Male, the pack leader and presumably father of the pups; Lone Ranger, a male probably two or three years old; Left Shoulder, a male similar to Lone Ranger but with a big gash in his left shoulder; and Scruffy, a yearling.

IWC: And the next year, in 1987?

LDM: It was the same array of adults, except that Scruffy showed up only for short periods the second summer. The 1986 pups were around the den only for a short time in summer 1987 and then disappeared.

IWC: Disappeared?

LDM: Yes, undoubtedly they dispersed. We've learned from our studies elsewhere with radio-collared wolves that most young wolves disperse from their natal packs between the ages of one and two years, some moving just next door and others traveling over five hundred miles away.

IWC: How many pups were born in 1987?

LDM: Five.

IWC: And in 1988?

LDM: Four pups, again produced by Mom. But this time there were only three other adults, and the alpha male had changed. The alpha male in 1986 and 1987 appeared to be the same individual, and in 1987 I noticed that one of his lower incisors (front teeth) was missing from his jaw. The alpha male in 1988 had all his lower incisors. The way he behaved both toward the other wolves and toward me made me believe that the new alpha male was Left Shoulder. I even thought I could see through his new fur the scar from the wound he had in 1986. A third adult, whom I named Whitey because she was so white and who must have been one of the 1987 pups, was a yearling. And the last adult, Gray Back, a male, appeared to be a yearling also, having been born in 1987.

IWC: So the pack had really changed composition considerably since the previous year?

LDM: Yes. And quite significantly I might add. Not only had five adults disappeared, but two of the 1987 pups had been recruited into the adult contingent.

IWC: What do you think happened to the five missing adults?

LDM: Some probably dispersed as I mentioned before, but three wolves were found dead in the general area over winter 1987–88.

IWC: What about the survival of the 1988 pack?

LDM: It was 100 percent. In 1989, the pack consisted of the four 1988 adults, plus the four 1988 pups who were now yearlings, and four new pups. But 1989 was a bizarre year in terms of what we know about wolf social organization. For much of the summer Mom, who was again the mother of the pups, and Whitey, who was now dominant to Mom, spent most of their time away from the alpha male, the two-year-old male Gray Back, and the four yearlings who all traveled together. The two females took care of the pups, while the other eight traveled on their own and were never seen as a group at the den. For a short period, one of the yearling females and a yearling male did associate with the two females and new pups around the den for a few days. In the fall, all twelve wolves finally got together.

IWC: Did all twelve survive over the winter?

LDM: That is one of the frustrating things about working in the High Arctic—it's impossible to determine what happens over the winter. By early October, it is dark twenty-four hours a day, and the sun does not appear again until March. However, in spring 1990 I was surprised to find that the pack had dwindled from twelve to three adults. The others could have dispersed or died. Only the alpha male, Whitey, and Mom remained. And Whitey was the new mother. Mom no longer had any pups so she became the grandmother. Furthermore, when I found the pack, Whitey had only one pup, about ten days old, and it was living in a pit or shallow depression in the ground, instead of in an enclosed den or rock cave.

IWC: You mean Whitey and her pup were right out in the open?

LDM: Yes, the pup was born in a depression dug into the ground, not a hole or a cave as they usually are. The mother Whitey was born in a big rock cave in 1987, but not her first pup. As the pup in the pit started getting larger, Whitey actually carried it to the rock cave. That's where she kept it for the next five weeks.

IWC: And after that?

LDM: Well, the most amazing thing happened then. When the pup was about seven weeks old and weighed only about ten pounds, it moved twenty miles with the pack.

IWC: That's incredible! I thought pups that size and age stayed in rendezvous sites, the nurseries, and play areas.

LDM: They usually do, although I have seen them travel a few miles from one rendezvous site to another. But nothing like this. Actually, there was a forerunner of this move when a week before, the adults had killed a musk-ox calf about eight miles away, and they took the pup to the kill. During the same trip, they even tried to attack some other musk-oxen with the pup along, and then returned to the cave den.

IWC: Did Whitey produce pups the next year, in 1991?

LDM: Yes. In 1991, Whitey bore her pups in the pit again, this time two pups, but she never did move them to the den in the cave.

IWC: You mean she left them in the pit all summer?

LDM: No. The pit in which they were born had a steep bank on each side of it, and when the pups were old enough to climb up the side of the pit and possibly fall over the bank, Whitey grabbed each one and carried it a mile to a pit at the base of a rock in the bottom of a valley. After two weeks, she moved them again to a rock ledge where they had a small cave, too small for any adult to crawl into. Five days later, she moved them again to another rock pile, this a much more elaborate one with several crannies and small caves. She left them there for most of the summer.

IWC: Whatever happened to the pups? Did they survive?

LDM: They survived into the fall, but as in all the other years, it is impossible to know what might have happened to them then. I never did see the 1990 pup in 1991. It was quite a runt, and conceivably did not make it through the winter.

IWC: It sounds as if the High Arctic can be a harsh place for a wolf.

LDM: Yes, it is harsh for every living being up there, including the wolves. But on the average, even though many individual animals fail to make it, the species survive and continue their unsparing struggle for existence.

An International Wolf Center Book

WOLVES

OF THE HIGH ARCTIC

Photographs by L. David Mech

THE HIGH ARCTIC

North of continental North America lies an area known as the High Arctic, a region characterized by islands the size of large states frozen into the Arctic Ocean and polar seas for ten months of the year. These islands stretch to within less than five hundred miles of the North Pole. Although barren and bleak, and dark day and night for five months of the year, the High Arctic still supports an interesting array of plant and animal life, sparse though it may be.

The arctic wolf, a white, medium-sized animal, inhabits the top of the world, the area between the north end of Canada's Hudson Bay and the North Pole, known as the High Arctic.

Overleaf: Most of the High Arctic remains covered with ice and snow year-round, and rugged mountain ranges poke up through the thick mantle of ice. Strange as it may sound, arctic wolves live in a desert world, for amount of precipitation defines a desert, and this part of the High Arctic averages only five inches of water a year.

Arctic wolf pups are born in late May or early June and must be tough enough to survive the constant arctic wind flowing off the ice fields and glaciers.

Despite winter windchill temperatures plummeting even farther than 100 degrees below zero, the arctic wolves patrol their bleak surroundings, searching for any kind of prey.

Even during summer, a season lasting
two to four weeks in mid-July, icebergs
and ice floes dot the frigid fjords sur-
rounding the High Arctic islands. Glacial
fronts gradually ooze their way down
broad valleys toward fjords and break off,
forming massive icebergs that spend their
lives floating for a few weeks in summer
and locked in for the rest of the year.

The polar bear patrols the frozen fjords, ever on the lookout for seals it can catch as they lie by their icy holes. Otherwise, finding an open crack large enough, the bear will plunge in and catch whatever else swims beneath the ice. Rarely found far from water or ice, the polar bear travels close to shore as it makes its long rounds in search of prey, and during the mating season, for a short-term partner.

Along some shores and in areas known as thermal oases, which are snow free for a few weeks in summer, short vegetation such as the arctic poppy pops up a few inches, just long enough to bloom, set seed, and die or resume dormancy for the long winter.

"Barren ground" rather than "tundra" is the preferred term for most of the area of the High Arctic that remains snow free during summer, while "tundra" refers to Arctic and Subarctic regions. Because it is frozen for ten to eleven months of the year, much of the land gets little chance to support tundra vegetation, in contrast with the "lush" Arctic and Subarctic a thousand miles to the south.

Purple saxifrage is hardy enough to thrive in the gravelly barrens. The plants begin pushing up through the snow in June and are blooming by the time the snow melts.

Arctic hare young, or leverets, are born grayish brown, which allows them to blend into their gravelly backgrounds and makes them much less visible to all the bird and mammal predators that seek to make meals of them.

The arctic hare is another herbivorous animal of the High Arctic. In the northernmost stretches of its range, there is not even time enough for the adults to change color, so they remain white year-round.

Rocky outcrops and gravelly ridges characterize the parts of the High Arctic that do manage to thaw in summer. Such features are often the only places where High Arctic animals can find shelter from the ever-present wind.

An adult arctic fox in summer coat still sports much of its white, furry winter pelt. Depending on just which month it happens to be, the arctic fox shows varying proportions of its black and white pelage. Cruising tirelessly over the barren ground with nose to the Earth, the fox sniffs any sign of bird, egg, insect, or mammal that might mean food.

The collared lemming, a mouselike sub-terranean creature, is one of the few plant-eating mammals inhabiting the High Arctic. Its number fluctuates greatly from year to year, and the animal is prey to all the carnivorous birds and mammals of the area, including the arctic wolf.

The short-tailed weasel, or ermine, ekes out a living in the High Arctic preying on lemmings, leverets, and small birds. Dashing from rock pile to rock pile, this tiny carnivore seems oblivious to the comings and goings of larger creatures.

Peary caribou, a small whitish form of the barren ground and woodland caribou, also inhabit the High Arctic. Like all caribou, it is a cousin of the reindeer. In many parts of the area, numbers of these elfin creatures remain relatively low.

Musk-oxen herds live sporadically throughout the High Arctic, garnering whatever vegetation they can as they wander nomadically. Their diet includes willows and sedges, as well as mosses and lichens, and during nine months of each year, musk-oxen and other herbivores must paw out vegetation from under a cover of snow. From time to time, musk-oxen fend off wolves, using their massive heads, horns, and hooves. Other times, a musk-ox falls prey to these arctic hunters.

During summer, long-tailed jaegers often pester wolves by diving to distract the wolves from ground nests. The eggs or nestlings would make only an hors d'oeuvre for a wolf, while the jaeger is defending a year of reproductive investment in them.

Seemingly oblivious to the cold and wind, a pack of arctic wolves rests on a ridgetop, sunning themselves. After five months of twenty-four-hour darkness from October through February, no doubt the spring sun feels especially good.

Overleaf: Hunting in the High Arctic, a wolf must travel far and wide over the barren grounds, ever searching for some kind of prey. At five to six miles per hour, the wolf can cover thirty or more miles a day. With prey as sparse as it is in such a region, the wolf must be able to keep up this pace just to find enough to eat.

A FAMILY OF ARCTIC WOLVES

Dave Mech, a wolf  biologist for over thirty years, befriended a pack of arctic wolves about six hundred miles south of the North Pole, and two hundred and fifty miles from the nearest Inuit village. Because these wolves had never been harassed by human beings, Mech was able to get close to them, find their dens, and live with the wolves for six summers since 1986.

When Dave Mech found the pack of wolves, there were seven adults and six pups. A pack is a family of related wolves: a pair of mature, breeding adults who are called the alpha male and female and who probably are unrelated, and their offspring of two or three annual litters. This wolf pack lived in an area of at least a thousand square miles on one of the islands in the High Arctic, summer and winter. They roamed and hunted a huge region.

The wolves feed on musk-oxen during winter and summer, as well as on other prey and food they scavenge. Eking a living off the barren, frozen island requires the wolves to be extra resourceful.

Although in winter the pack usually travels together, a wolf may temporarily stray from the group, and prowl on its own.

During summer, individual pack members often travel on their own. This allows the pack to cover a much larger area in search of scarce food.

To contact other packmates who also are traveling an area, an arctic wolf need only stop to howl. Over open ground, the wolf's howl travels for miles, and its pack members will return the call, allowing the whole pack to assemble.

For three summers, the pack used a cave at the base of a rocky outcrop in which to bear their pups. Carbon-dating the wolf-chewed bones around the cave entrance indicated that the den had been used over a period of at least seven hundred years.

The alpha male dominates a subordinate wolf by standing stiffly, with raised tail, growling, and threatening the subordinate. Such displays allow each wolf to know its place in the pack's social hierarchy, and keep daily life relatively harmonious. Fighting within a pack is rare. Around the rock-cave den, three members of the pack mixed it up in a social display. Frequent interactions among pack members probably help bond each individual to the pack.

Although pesky at times, these two pups
were usually able to get a drink from their
mother whenever they tried hard enough.

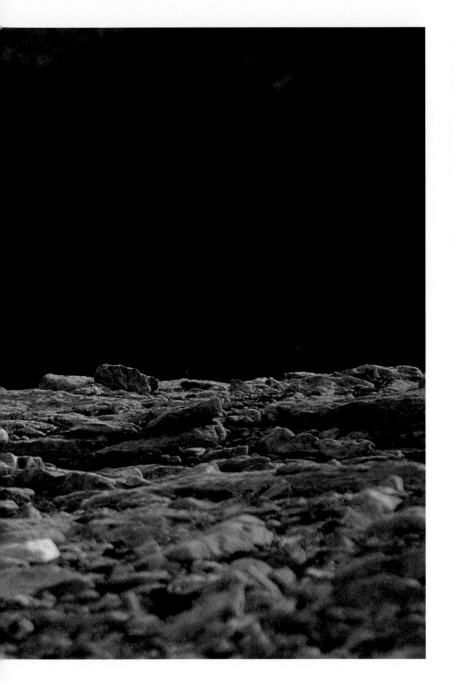

In later years, the wolves used other dens and sometimes produced pups in shallow pits dug into the earth. The mother wolf then would nurse her pups on top of the ground.

A four-week-old pup almost resembles a kitten. At this age, pups rarely stray far from their den, but their curiosity grows daily. Even when older, pups like to frequent the den, though sometimes they may wander as far away as a quarter to a half mile. Young wolf pups tire easily. After a short trip or a bout of play, they like to lie around and watch their packmates. Any unusual sight or sound around the den grabs a pup's attention and may result in an exploratory mission.

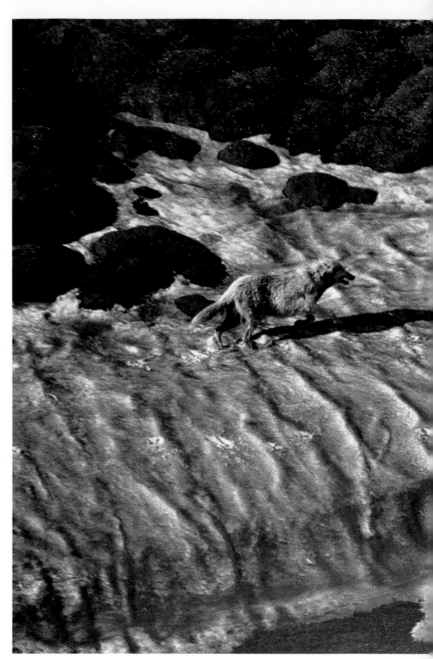

Ever watchful, each wolf scans the large vistas of its territory, looking for any sign of prey, enemies, and things arousing interest. Prey primarily are large and small plant-eaters, enemies most often mean other wolves, and things arousing interest include humans. All scats and urine—indeed any foreign odor or sign of an intruding wolf—elicit intense examination.

If a strange wolf is sensed, the whole pack streaks off in pursuit. If at all possible, the animals chase the intruder until they catch it. A wolf that intrudes into the pack's territory may pay for it. The stranger may meet with a fatal attack. After such a wounding, a wolf will die outright or within a few hours. These interactions help keep a pack's territory free of competitors for the sparse food supply.

Overleaf: Although life proves hard for the arctic wolf, sleep is also important. These wolves sometimes slept for twenty hours straight.

DENNING AND
PUP PRODUCTION

One of the most inter- esting aspects in the

life in the wolf is den- ning and pup produc-

tion. Wolves usually are so sensitive and secretive about their pups that it

is rare to have an opportunity to observe the interactions between the pups

and adults. With this High Arctic pack, however, their lack of fear of hu-

mans allowed biologist Dave Mech to watch them daily and record what-

ever information he wanted.

Most of the adult pack members spent their time near the mouth of the den, although the alpha female remained right with the pups for much of their first three weeks of life.

The cave at the base of this massive rock outcrop, which served as the wolves' den for three years, provided excellent shelter for the pups.

The rest of the pack members received the rapt attention of Whitey and her two pups. Born in 1987, Whitey was the daughter of Mom and had become the breeding female in 1990. Mom, who was the mother of the pack's offspring during 1986–1988, remained with the pack as grandmother.

On short trips away from the den itself, the mother usually kept the pups near rocky crevices and cracks to where they could escape in case of danger.

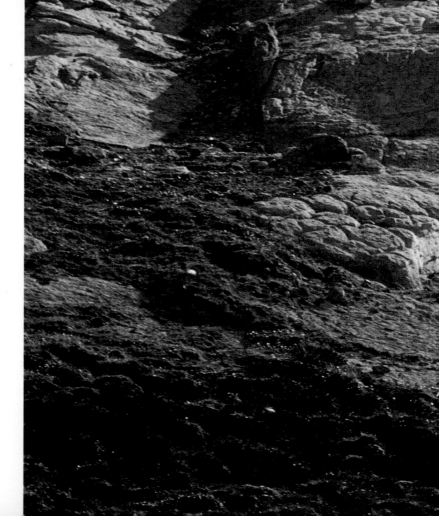

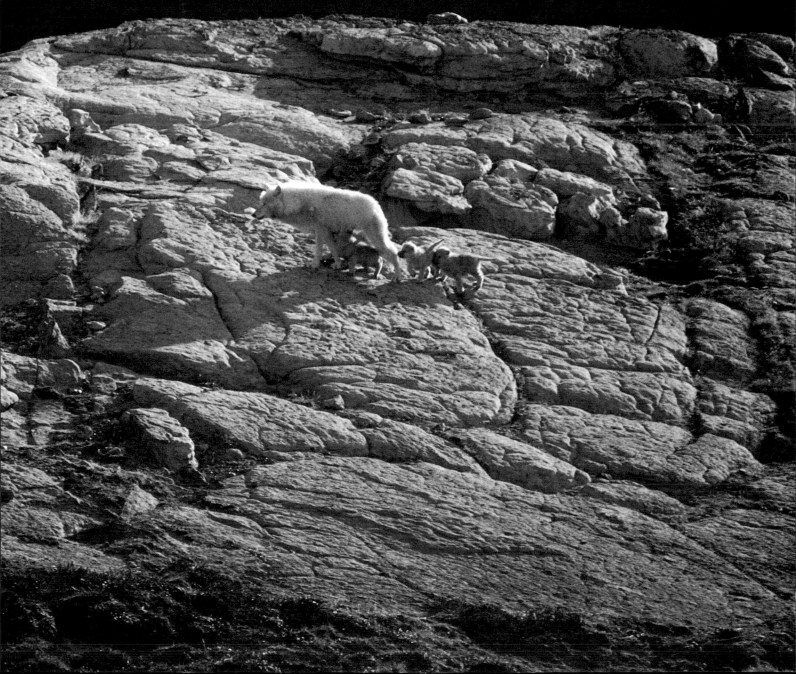

Blackface often strolled around the den area with one or more of the pups. The gut contents of musk-oxen may have stained this wolf's face as he fed on the carcasses.

The alpha pair one year, Whitey and Blackface stuck together much of the time when they were away from the pups.

One of the main ways adults carry food to pups is in their stomachs, and the pups soon learn how to dislodge it. As any adult approached a pup, the pup would jump up and lick at the adult's mouth, trying to trigger the adult to regurgitate half-digested food to it. Even Whitey, the nursing mother, was besieged continually for food.

With larger litters of pups, it helps to have more adult pack members to find, catch, and carry the food home to the pups. All pack members help raise, feed, and care for the pups.

71

When pups approach an adult without food, the adult must be firm in conveying to the pups that it cannot feed them. It does so by bowling the pups over and pinning them to the ground. The pups continue to paw at the adult and beg food from it. With so many pups to contend with, the adult can be overwhelmed. The only hope is to try to escape from the frisky, begging pups. If the adult hesitates, it is once again besieged and will have to run far enough away to ditch the pups.

The usual litter size of mature wolves is four to six. So many pups, however, keep the adult pack members especially busy trying to feed them.

One year, only one pup was born. It was Whitey's first time as a mother, which might explain her small litter size.

CARE OF THE PUPS

Taking care of wolf pups is not an easy job. Although all pack members help with the task, especially the feeding, the greatest part of the effort falls on the pups' mother. Not only must she nurse the pups, but also she usually is the only one who may pick up the pups and move them in case of danger or if they are unruly. Because the pups are extremely rambunctious, it is all the mother can do to keep them in line.

All the pack's adults tend to the pups while around the den. However, much of the time most adults are away hunting, leaving the pups with their mother and/or a babysitter. The pups' fuzzy fur is so dense that the animals can withstand the cold high arctic wind as well as rain and snow.

Pups like to scamper among the rocks of their barren homeland, crawling in and out of the cracks and crevices.

A five-week-old pup peers out from a favorite sunny spot it has chosen for rest.

If a pup strays too far away or heads for danger, mother simply picks it up in her mouth.

Even when barely able to walk, wolf pups find rocky slopes of great interest. Mother, as always, keeps a watchful eye as her pups explore their new world.

All the wolf's sharp teeth surround the tiny pup, but the mother is able to gauge her bite so as not to harm it.

With the pup firmly in her mouth, the mother can carry it to wherever she deems safest. Wolves have been known to carry their pups for a mile or more when changing dens.

Nursing often starts when pups begin
playing around their mother. They crawl
all over her and eventually make their
way to her nipples. As the pups compete
for a good grip, they struggle with one
another and show their competitiveness
through raised tails. Often the mother
wolf prefers to nurse the pups standing
up, so she may arise and force them to do
so.

The pups' struggle continues as they strive to balance on their hind legs while reaching up for their mother's teats. Locking their legs around their mother's helps the pups to keep their balance and their grip. Nursing bouts last about five minutes. If the pups want to continue nursing against their mother's will, the mother simply starts running off, and the pups must let go.

A mother wolf shares some choice prey parts with her pups. Although adults bring much of their food to the pups in their stomachs, they also begin to carry parts of prey back in their mouths.

Besides transferring food to pups mouth to mouth, adults also greet pups by licking their mouths. Even between adults this is a standard greeting.

PUPS AT PLAY

One of the most typical characteristics of wolf pups is their playfulness. They play by themselves, they play with each other, they play with adults, and they play with toys such as bones, fur, and feathers. Play serves several functions. It allows the pups to exercise their rapidly developing muscles, helps them test each other's strength as well as their own, and allows them to practice behavior they will need to use as adults in order to survive.

Pups make good use of the sand flats of a river bed on which to gambol.

Nose-to-nose encounters sometimes precede a quick spring-away, followed by a chase. Both very young pups and elderly adults play this game.

A month-old pup peers intently at a playing littermate before scampering down to join in.

As two pups wrestle, they develop muscle tone and test both their own and their partner's strength and skill.

An old arctic fox tail becomes a perfect
toy for a pair of pups. They fight over it
relentlessly, play tag with it, and treat it
like a prey animal. The highest use of a
fox-tail toy for wolf pups is as the prize in
a tug-of-war. Tug-of-war is one of the
most useful skills a growing pup can develop because as an adult it will need to
employ the tactic in competing for food.

Adult and pup pause from a bout of play and greet each other nose to nose. This common greeting is performed constantly and, no doubt, helps further the bonds of these highly social animals. Adolph Murie, the first biologist to observe wild wolves closely, remarked that the strongest impression that remained with him was the friendliness of the wolves toward their packmates.

A lone pup without littermates must occupy itself when adults are away, and has much fewer chances for play. Consequently, it is possible that the animal may develop a different personality than pups raised with littermates.

A pair of littermates scramble through the cottongrass in a game of tag.

One pup plays the attacker; the other, the
victim.

Tables turn, and the victim attacks.

After long bouts of play, pups may stop and begin a social howl. So, too, in adults, howling often follows an intense social ceremony.

TO FEED THE FAMILY

Wolf pups in the High Arctic must grow and develop fast during the quick summer. By October, darkness has set in, and the pups will not see the sun again until late February. To survive over winter, the pups must gain as much weight as possible as quickly as possible. This takes great amounts of meat. Wolves will eat any kind of food they can scavenge or catch, including seals, lemmings, birds, and hares. However, in the High Arctic, a high percentage of their food must come from musk-oxen.

When the whole pack sets out on a hunt,
it is usually for musk-oxen rather than for
smaller prey. To find a herd, the pack often must travel twenty or thirty miles. As
wolves hunt, their senses allow the
animals to scan hundreds of square miles
for the scent, sight, or sound of prey they
can catch or of food they can scavenge.

When away from the rest of the pack, the alphas often howl to help reassemble the group.

When on their long hunts, pack members show no fear or hesitancy about wading right into a river or, if necessary, swimming across.

Once a herd of musk-oxen is found, the wolves approach slowly and quietly. Then a quick rush may panic the herd. Running prey are safer to attack. Usually, however, the herd stops when the wolves close in; the wolves then face a formidable front. Often musk-oxen form a circle of defense—rumps in, horns and front hooves out. Their simple lines of defense can prove equally impenetrable. More often than not, the predators must turn tail, abandon their hopes, and then travel many more miles in search of another herd. When they do find another herd, the wolves again try to take advantage of unevenness in terrain and to sneak as close to the musk-oxen as possible.

When the musk-oxen finally detect the wolves and flee, the wolves put on a mighty burst of speed to catch them. As they close in, the wolves look for vulnerable members of the herd.

Calves are easier to catch and kill than adults, so the wolves concentrate on them. The wolves attack the calf wherever they can, usually around the head and rump.

After bringing down the calf, the wolves immediately begin to feed. They try to open the abdomen and seek out the internal organs. Even pulling apart a musk-ox calf after it is finally caught and killed takes a great deal of work. By pulling, tugging, chewing, and tearing, wolves manage to cut through parts of the carcass.

Other pack members join in, and their long-awaited feast begins, often days after the pack started out to hunt. The wolves will return to the pups with full stomachs, bounty to share. If a kill is large enough, a wolf may carry off a piece and bury it for later use — perhaps a meal after an unsuccessful hunt.

A quick trip to a nearby river allows the wolf to wash its bloody face and slake its thirst.

Overleaf: After covering many miles each day and perhaps chasing many prey, Blackface, the alpha male, rests. Fall will approach in August. Often, pups or subordinate pack members perish over winter. However, chances are much better that these two founders of the changing pack, Blackface and Whitey, will be around in spring to try again.

READINGS

Readers will uncover a wealth of facts and photographs about the wolf in the following books:

Allen, D. L. 1979. *The Wolves of Minong: Their Vital Role in a Wild Community.* Houghton Mifflin Company, Boston.

Bibikov, D. I. 1988. *Der Wolf.* A. Ziemsen Verlag, Wittenberg Lutherstodt.

Boitani, L. 1987. *Dalla Parte del Lupo.* L'Airone di Giorgio Mondadori e Associati Spa, Milano.

Harrington, F. H., and P. C. Paquet (editors). 1982. *Wolves of the World.* Noyes Publications, Park Ridge, New Jersey.

Klinghammer, E. (editor). 1979. *The Behavior and Ecology of Wolves.* Garland STPM Press, New York, London.

Mech, L. D. 1988. *The Arctic Wolf: Living with the Pack.* Voyageur Press, Stillwater, Minnesota.

Mech, L. D. 1991. *The Way of the Wolf.* Voyageur Press, Stillwater, Minnesota.

Mech, L. D. 1970, reprint 1981. *The Wolf: Ecology and Behavior of an Endangered Species.* University of Minnesota Press, Minneapolis, Minnesota.

Murie, A. 1944. *The Wolves of Mount McKinley.* Fauna of the National Parks of the United States. Fauna Series No. 5. U.S. Government Printing Office.

National Geographic Video. 1988. *White Wolf.* National Geographic Society, Washington, D.C.

Peterson, R. O. 1977. *Wolf Ecology and Prey Relationships on Isle Royale.* National Park Service Scientific Monograph Series No. 11.

Savage, Candace. 1988. *Wolves.* Sierra Club Books, San Francisco, California.

Walberg, K. I. 1987. *Ulven.* Grondahl & Sons, Forlag A. S., Olso.

Zimen, E. 1981. *The Wolf: A Species in Danger.* Delacorte, New York.

Young readers might start their quest after wolves in these books:

Field, Nancy, and Corliss Karasov. 1991. *Discovering Wolves.* Dog-Eared Publications, Middleton, Wisconsin.

Johnson, Sylvia A., and Alica Aamodt. 1985. *Wolf Pack: Tracking Wolves in the Wild.* Lerner Publications Company, Boston.

Robinson, Sandra Chisholm. 1989. *Wonder of Wolves.* Denver Museum of Natural History with Roberts Rhinehart, Inc., Niwot, Colorado.

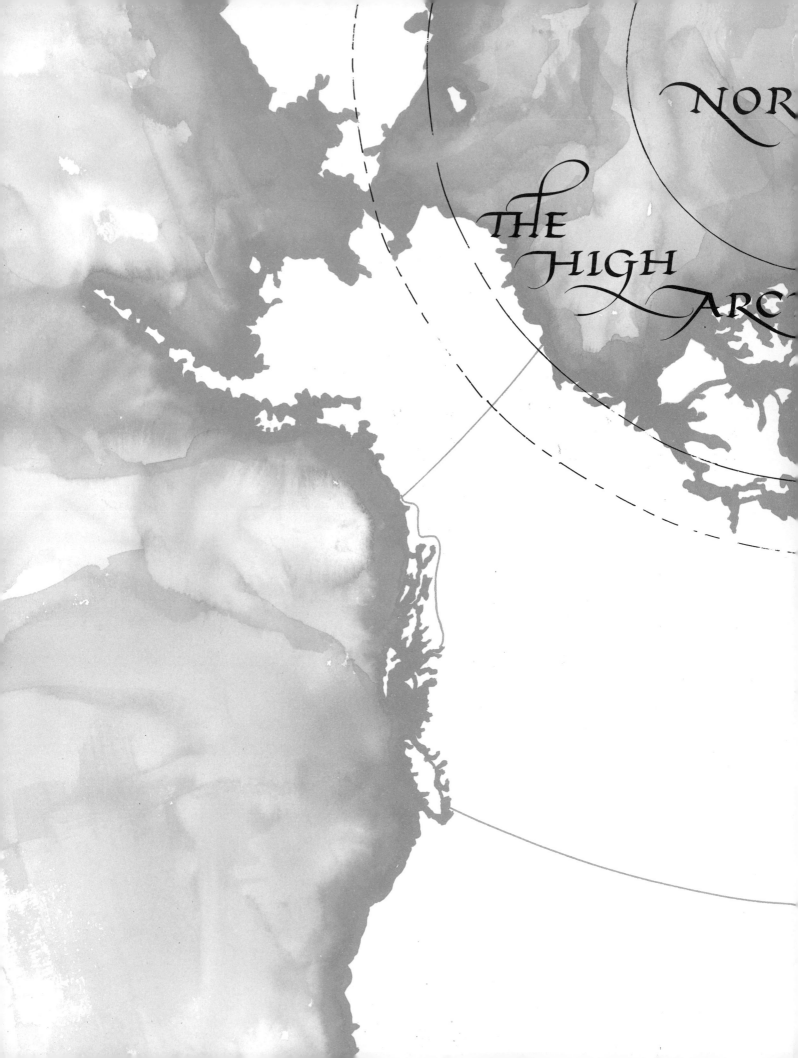

NOR

THE
HIGH
ARC